Contents

Forward

"They're certainly entitled to think that, and they're entitled to full respect for their opinions... but before I can live with other folks I've got to live with myself. The one thing that doesn't abide by majority rule is a person's conscience."

— Harper Lee

I was both excited and slightly unsure about writing the foreword for Rome Za's new book. Certainly, I felt I knew him as well as anyone, meeting him as a patient in my office, and then watching his remarkable evolution over the following years. Yet, it is always challenging to define a person, their characteristics, and ultimately their essence in a only a few sentences.

There is one word that comes to mind though when I think of Rome. It is the the one intangible that makes him a successful leader, both in business and in his personal life, as well as my most trusted friend and business partner. That words is INTEGRITY. Before I explain how it is that he is the embodiment of that word let me tell you how it is that we first met.

Rome first walked into my office in the winter of 2010, seeking treatment for injuries to his neck and back. Having been to many doctors and having been diagnosed with multiple herniated discs, no one was able to help eliminate his debilitating pain. This was not unusual for me. Being in practice at the time for close to 15 years, I was used to being the last stop before surgery. It is something I had seen thousands of times. People would come and get better and then move on with their lives.

Rome was no ordinary patient though. At the time, he was coming to my office three times a week, exercising daily, and altering his diet to push his healing process to a new level while finishing his studies for a nursing degree. In just a few months, he would graduate, start to make money, and be able to help people. At least that's what I had thought the game plan was for him.

Then I saw something that was unique and amazing to me. I saw in him a burning desire to shape others into the best version of themselves. He was at a crossroads though because he did not see nursing as the best means to achieve that. Most people would not have the courage to walk away after being so invested. Rome is not "most people" though. He made the tough choice to walk away from nursing, knowing it ran on a on a model of care he did not believe in. With a heap of school loans, a guaranteed paycheck, and his peer respect in the balance, he chose the path less traveled. One filled with uncertainty and risk. He chose to pursue his passion of helping others by opening up a Jiu-Jitsu school where he could help people improve their health, as well as give them the discipline and confidence to overcome any other challenge in their lives.

Yes. You read that correctly. After years studying and thousands of dollars in debt, he made the decision to open his own business. Not one in health care, not one that centered on his whole college experience, but a mma gym that focused on jujitsu. Now that to some might sound crazy and to some it might sound courageous; however, it was just Rome being Rome. A man that creates his own destiny. One who follows his heart.

So should I have been surprised when a couple years later he said he was closing the gym and moving to Costa Rica? Hell no. Because it was never about what was easiest, or what brought him the most money, it was always about what was the RIGHT thing to do.

Now I couldn't be more grateful that Rome has chosen to share his blueprint on how you can have that same power to take the leap and grow. Because growing can be tough. It takes the ability to make hard choices. It means looking into your soul and knowing that the right decisions can often be the most difficult. And that sometimes one needs to suffer and battle to make that change. Because what else is there? Shuffling through life, not taking chances, not pursuing your dream, is not the path that Rome paves..

This book will give you many principles on how to approach your life. To be happy on the deepest of levels, to achieve anything that you want to obtain, with a sense of purpose. The beauty is that every single person, no matter how "successful" they are can improve their quality of life with the advice in this book..

After 20 years of running a successful chiropractic and nutrition practice, having a great wife and two wonderful kids, I thought I had it all. And yet, I myself am transformed by this book. Taking the art of being truthful to a new level, learning how to truly listen, to others and to myself, I recognize I was happily going through the motions of life. Yes, I was helping people, but was I really living my life to my fullest potential? Was I making the tough decisions I needed to make to grow? No. I wasnt challenging myself and choosing a "safe" path. Falsely believing I was doing my best, when really it was just the tip of the iceberg. So I looked in the mirror, and guided by Rome, made the tough choices and that has made all the difference. The sense of joy and accomplishment I now possess as a result is priceless.

This book will help you cut through the superficial and grasp the inner peace of knowing you are achieving your best.

It will also show you the experience of a man who has struggled and fought his share of emotional demons along the way. Nobody is exempt from hardship, and the beauty of this book is that it is written, not from an idealistic representation, but from a place of experience, a philosophy molded on learning what the true measures are needed to step forward and achieve anything you desire in this world.

So back to INTEGRITY. The word integrity can be defined as "one of strong moral conviction and honor" as well as 'the state of being whole and undivided." I could not define Rome any better than that. This is the way that he lives every moment of his life and it has allowed him to accomplish incredible things. .

The book you hold in your hands will present new and challenging ideas. Yet know that regardless of what your dream is, the tools that Rome presents will allow you to move courageously and unwaveringly forward along your path.

Dr. Ian Stern

Total Wellness Chiropractic

Chapter 1: Before We Begin

Awakening the Warrior Within

At 26, everyone thought I was living the dream. I had a mixed martial arts studio of about a hundred students, a brand new, black BMW, nice clothes, a beautiful family, and an amazing girlfriend. From the outside looking in, I had the perfect life. No one knew we were barely making ends meet, or that there was something deep down inside of me longing to be freed.

I was living a life of quiet desperation. I didn't know what to do. Well, truthfully, deep down inside, I *did* know what to do. I just couldn't think about it. I couldn't talk about. I definitely couldn't *do* anything about it.

Why couldn't I do anything about it, you ask? First of all, my fear of criticism was crippling. Everybody thought I had a dream life. I wanted to scream out, "My purpose is elsewhere! This dream life you guys think I'm living isn't *my* dream. I want to do something else. I want to keep growing! I don't want to just be a martial arts instructor. Being a martial arts instructor isn't my huge, big, lifelong purpose! That's only a *part* of who I am." But how could I stand up and say that when my life was so great? I knew most people wouldn't understand.

My life changed after a chance meeting with an Amazonian shaman. We immediately hit it off, and he invited me to sit in his ceremonial circle. The very next day after that sacred, reverent experience, I knew exactly what was missing from my life. For starters, I was living in the wrong place.

I felt a strong pull towards Costa Rica. Why Costa Rica? Well, I'd visited when I was 21 years old and absolutely love it. Of course I was a different person back then, but as Costa Rica had had such a profound impact on me, I'd always wanted to go back. The very next day after the idea hit me, I immediately made it official with my then-girlfriend and proposed. Then, I shared my thoughts with her. I said, "Hey, do you want to go check out Costa Rica? I'm kind of getting tired of New York." Being the awesome person she is, my fiancée supported me and agreed to seize the opportunities of a life in Costa Rica.

One month after that conversation, my wife and I visited Costa Rica. We loved it! It was magical. We met incredible people, connected with the land, and soon realized that a more simple life was the life we wanted to live. Our relationship grew stronger, and we were certain Costa Rica was the ideal place for our personal and professional development. We'd surround ourselves with like-minded people and flourish.

Visiting Costa Rica gave me a definite, chief aim. I wanted to move there as quickly as possible. There was only one problem: I was in debt. *A lot* of debt. I had student loans, business loans, credit card bills, household bills, and a car note for my BMW! We'd invested well over six figures into the studio, and now I was thinking of moving away from it. What was I going to do? I was broke and had definite ties to New York, but Costa Rica was in my sights. I just had to figure out how to make the move happen.

Like a carefully tended garden, my passion for making the move grew day by day, minute by minute. I wanted to live in Costa Rica, and I became intensely focused on making it a reality.

And then, one day, an amazing opportunity presented itself: I found a way to earn another income. A buddy of mine introduced me to selling stuff online. As you know, using the Internet to generate income allows you to work anywhere with a Wi-Fi or Ethernet connection, so I'd be able to make money from anywhere!

I had a lot of fears surrounding my new opportunity. I thought, *Whoa! This seems too good to be true.*

People are really making money doing this? And they don't have to go teach six hours of classes? I knew I at least had to explore the option, but would I really be able to do it? I'd never worked on the Internet before. Would I be good enough for this amazing chance of a lifetime?

Luckily, my passion was stronger than my fear. I seized that passion and held on to it for dear life. My desire to move, try something new, and live my best life greatly outweighed any fears about possible failures. The fear of staying where I was, changing nothing, and sticking with what had become comfortable for me was the scariest fear of all. I *had* to do it, or live with the regret of inaction for the rest of my life. So, I looked into the opportunity. I started learning about the possibilities of online sales. After concluding that it would be foolish for me to pass up, I committed. Once I made my commitment, I became dedicated to making our move happen in a year and a half or less.

I had a five-year-old son, a pregnant wife, and my 80-pound pit bull living in a tiny, one-bedroom, basement apartment in Brooklyn, New York. As I said, we were barely making ends meet. Sometimes I had to borrow money from friends just to pay my rent at the studio.

I worked at the gym from 4:00-10:00 p.m. every single day. Whether I was teaching my five classes then signing up students, or signing up students then teaching classes, I was there *every single day* until 10:00 p.m. I was the only trainer there, and it was *my* studio. So it was all on me.

After leaving the studio, I'd take about 30 minutes to shower and eat. Then, at around 10:30 p.m. *every single night*, I'd get started on the grinding, the learning, the implementing, the testing, and the pushing until 4:00 a.m. *every single morning*. I would pore over information, learning the things necessary to help me become the person I needed to be in order to move to Costa Rica. With my family, my livelihood, and sense of purpose driving me, I was grinding. And I'd keep grinding.

I maintained this schedule for more than 365 days straight. While everyone was sleeping, I was grinding. While everyone was partying, I was grinding. While everyone was out drinking, I was grinding. While my friends and teammates were all training, I was grinding. Even through sickness–and man, I got sick *a lot* thanks to the daily physical strain of my jiu jitsu teachings and training–I WAS GRINDING.

At a certain point, I stopped training jiu jitsu. Don't get me wrong, I loved my martial arts studio and students, and jiu jitsu was my first love. I loved my life and the people in it. I was ok with who I had become. I just hated who I *hadn't* become. I knew I had a bigger, higher purpose, and if I continued with more of the same, I'd never fully realize it. I became completely devoted to doing what I needed to do to make my move happen, so jiu jitsu training took a backseat.

And so, I was grinding. It was a different kind of grind. It was a hunger like I'd never felt before. I didn't go out. I didn't hang. Once a week, I'd meet with other like-minded individuals in a mastermind group. None of us really knew how to use the Internet to make money, but we worked together to figure out what the hell we needed to do to meet our goals. We knew how to talk to people on Facebook, but we had to learn all other necessary skills from scratch.

My same old fears and mental blockages kept coming up. I thought, *Am I enough? Will I ever learn all this information? Will this ever happen for me? Will I ever move to Costa Rica? Am I going to be stuck in New York for the rest of my life?*

Despite my fears, something inside me began to open its eyes. The *warrior* inside me began to awaken. No, he was *forced* to awaken. The warrior in me realized I couldn't let any amount of fear keep me from actualizing my dreams and my destiny.

This book will provide you with the blueprint and philosophies necessary to awaken the warrior inside of *you*. I'll tell you all about what I had to change and who I had to become in order to awaken the warrior and realize my purpose. Everything in this book is coming straight from my heart, and my hope is you'll use it to help change your life.

I originally wasn't going to write this book. However, something higher, something stronger, something more divine overruled. I *had* to share my message; I *had* to share my love. I had to share my story so it would help to inspire and transform others. I had to put these words out there to resonate and encourage you to be the best version of yourself. I want to help you become the best parent, the best lover, the best businessman, hell, the best damn worldwide steward you can be!

Now is the time to seriously commit to being your best self. I want you to awaken the warrior inside. You have talents to share with the world. You have a gift waiting to come out.

We all have a gift. Each of our gifts is special. Each of our gifts is beautiful. Each of our gifts is *powerful*. And each and every one of us holds a small piece to the amazing universal puzzle. By not becoming the best you and sharing your gift, you aren't just cheating yourself and your family. You're selling the whole *planet* short! You're selling me and everyone else short by chipping out and being a punk ass bitch! Imagine how much could we accomplish as a planet if we were all being our best selves!

Let him breathe. Let *her* breathe. Give your warrior life. Step into your warrior. Awaken the warrior within. Let him or her come out!

Stay tuned. This book is going to change your life.

Consciously Evolving by Any Means Necessary

On December 9th, 2014, a year and two months after I committed to changing my life, we moved to Costa Rica. We actually made it! But my journey didn't end after the move. After changing my environment, the real work of self-improvement, self-discovery, and evolution had to begin. I would continue to grow into a better man for myself, my family, and the world–by any means necessary.

This book is a recorded history of my successes, failures, and lessons learned from the last few years. This is a history of the thousands of books I've read, the dozens of courses I've taken, and the many, many coaching programs I've done. It's a testimonial borne with self-reflection, pain, and struggle. I'm very grateful for all of the opportunities and challenges the universe has presented to me, and I'm thankful I get to share them with you.

As I reflect on my story up to this point, I'm reminded of a quote from *The Teachings of Buddha*: "Thousands of candles can be lighted from a single candle, and the life of the single candle will not be shortened. Happiness never decreases by being shared." I lose nothing from helping others, and I gain the satisfaction of knowing I've helped someone start a purposeful journey. I want to share my story with you. I want to connect with you in hopes of helping you avoid some of the pitfalls I fell into as I awakened the warrior within. I lay myself bare before you, dear reader. Keep my words in mind as you awaken your warrior and consciously evolve on your path to success.

Let's start with a few truths and tips: First and foremost, know that building your life upon a weak belief system is essentially setting yourself up for a huge crash. Keep your goals and the motivation behind those goals in mind, because this is what will keep you going when times get rough. Find something to believe in, be prepared for the long haul, and put in work daily. Create a daily schedule that will allow you to both take care of business and spend time with those who matter most.

Secondly, stop multitasking. Contrary to popular belief, multitasking is the enemy of all high-level productivity. Focus intently and implement one strategy at a time so you'll be able to pinpoint exact cause and effect, and so you do your best work on every task.

Thirdly, remember you're in it for the long haul. It takes 30 to 60 days on average to create a new habit. I know you may have heard some people say it only takes 21 days to create a new habit, but in my experience, it takes 30 to 60 days.

So, you spend 30 to 60 days creating a new habit for yourself. Does that mean your new task is going to be easy after it becomes a habit? Not at all! You'll continue to have a daily internal battle. Part of you will want to continue with your new improvements, while another part will resist the changes you've made. Exercise your mind, spirit, and body. Continue to consciously evolve.

Fourthly, follow the Mastermind/Accountability Principle. I learned about the Mastermind Principle from Napoleon Hill in *Think and Grow Rich*. Mr. Hill recommends bringing together people with common goals. In my case, I wanted to live around people who were focused on living the life of their dreams while maintaining honesty, integrity, and love.

What are the benefits of having a personal mastermind group of like-minded people, you ask?

- Your group keeps you true to yourself and holds you accountable for the goals you set and promises you make. Accountability partners are HUGE! They make it so you're no longer answering to and lying to yourself like you've probably been doing your whole life. There's no gray area with a mastermind group; it's only black and white. Your group will ask, "Did you complete your task/meet your goal?" You'll have to respond with either a yes or no. No one wants to hear, "I kind of did it."

  When you have someone to answer to who doesn't want to hear your excuses, what happens? You make sure to get shit done right away! The only thing you really and truly own in this world is your word. You can give your word freely, but no one will want it if you don't follow through. In a mastermind group, no one wants to be the one to drop the ball.

- Celebrations are a lot more fun with someone who gets it! If you crush a huge goal and share it with someone who has no clue as to what you're talking about, your high will become a little deflated. You won't enjoy the experience as much sharing it with someone who doesn't really care. And of course you don't want to celebrate alone. So, include people

who understand your grind and your journey. It will make your triumphs so much more enjoyable.

- Mastermind groups point out your weaknesses and help you fix them. Everyone in your group has a different path and different areas that need improvement. Your group will help to pinpoint shortcomings and help you better yourself.

  Some members of your group will be better at sales than you. Some will be better at creating a positive, action-oriented mindset. Some group members are going to be better at maintaining fitness goals. And of course, you'll be better at something than other members. A great mastermind utilizes everyone's strengths and improves upon everyone's weaknesses. The key is bringing together people who might be very different from each other, but who are on similar journeys. Mastermind group members have a common purpose, know each other's goals, and will help each other find success a lot faster.

  My fifth tip is to create reminders for yourself and place them wherever you spend an extended amount of time. Have your reminders in your house, car, wallet, and work space. Doing so ensures you'll always have your definite, chief aim implanted into your mind. I have my reminders and subgoals all over my room. I have them in my car; I carry them in my wallet. Because of my reminders, I constantly know exactly what I want to achieve. When the opportunity comes up to get something done, I seize it. I get things done because I know at all times *what* I want to get done.

So sure, set up reminders everywhere. But what kind of reminders? How do you know what you need to do to accomplish your goals? How do you get where you want to go if you *don't know* where you want to go? This is a question you need to ask yourself. People are always complaining about not getting where they want to go in life. But do you actually know what you want? And how specific are your wants?

Your current goal might be to get rich. That's not specific enough. You can't simply say, "I want to get rich" and call it a goal. You'll need to set very specific, detailed, step-by-step subgoals to accomplish your chief aim. Before you do that, read more to learn about the transformative philosophies that changed my and hundreds of my students' lives. After learning these philosophies, you'll need to keep them all over as reminders to help keep you on point and headed towards the life you want to lead.

Tools of the Trade

Bruce Lee once said, "Absorb what is useful, discard what is not, add what is uniquely your own."

During my years of consciously evolving and awakening the warrior within, I've stumbled upon ancient tools that have been huge catalysts in my evolution.

I'm going to share the foundational tools of my trade with you. I'm also going to teach you how and when to use them.

Now, every profession has specific tools. Warriors have swords and spheres. Carpenters have hammers and nails. Builders have bricks and cement. Doctors have stethoscopes and thermometers. I'm going to share with you the tools that will help you in any and every profession. You're going to have the strongest tools ever given to humanity.

These tools have been around for thousands and thousands of years. They not only yield amazing, incredible results in the physical plane, they'll have a great impact on your mental and spiritual planes as well.

Now, let's get started.

Stepping into the Void (Meditation)

I first heard about meditation when I was a child. But back then, anyone I asked essentially told me meditation was a weird thing only Asian people did. I finally tried it for myself when I was 23 years old, the summer I dropped out of college and opened my MMA Academy.

The first day I tried meditation, I thought it wasn't working. But I'd already decided that if other people could find inner peace and complete harmony with *their* environments, then so could I!

So, I started reading. I read every book I could find on meditation and stepping into the void.

After reading all I could read, I tried to practice what I'd read. I'd sit down, show up, and do the work. At first I just sat and sat...and sat. I sat for an hour, an hour and a half, an hour and fourty-five minutes at a time. I played around with different breathing and visualization techniques. I played around with so many different variables and tried dozens upon dozens of different types of meditations.

One day, everything just clicked. It took *a lot* of practice to get to that point, but I finally stepped into the void. Time and space no longer existed. I felt myself disappear. By Earth's measure of time, I was gone for about 45 minutes or so. When it was over, I felt rejuvenated! It was almost as if someone had recharged my batteries. It was the most incredible feeling. I was euphoric for hours after that experience.

I couldn't find that feeling again the next day. I would feel a glimmer of the void, then I'd lose it. Then I'd feel it again. Then I'd lose it. It was a continuous back and forth, but I kept going. It was an incredible thing to stick to, and I was committed. I'd experienced what stepping into the void felt like and I wanted more. I wanted to recharge my batteries again and again.

Meditation wasn't simply giving me more inner peace and complete harmony with my environment. My meditations were also making the people around me happier because of my increasingly positive energy field.

Whenever I go to events, I run to my room and meditate for fifteen to twenty minutes. I do all types of meditations; guided meditations, mantra meditations, silent meditations, and visual meditations, to name a few. They all work in amazing ways and unlock different things inside of me. I don't like any one technique over the other, so I try every type of meditation I know!

Now I'll teach you techniques for both premeditation and meditation that have immensely helped me throughout my journey. I learned these two techniques from a combination of several different courses and various yoga instructors. I'm sure these techniques have been used before, but I had to recreate and personalize them for myself in order to wholeheartedly understand.

First, sit down in complete silence. Turn off all phones, computers, tablets, and other electronic devices. Then, cross your feet and put your right hand inside your left hand with your thumbs touching.

I started out meditating by the wall because it helped to keep my back straight. It used to cause me pain to keep my back straight without support, and the wall made it a lot easier. If you can't comfortably sit with your back straight, I recommend you use a wall. If even the wall doesn't help, sit in a chair with your legs uncrossed and feet touching the floor.

Let's begin our premeditation. Unless you're sitting in a chair, you should be in a crossed-legged position. Close your eyes. Take in a deep breath for four seconds. Fill yourself with air from your stomach to your chest to your throat, all the way up to the tippy top of your head. Hold your breath for four more seconds. Then, slowly breathe out for another four seconds. Be still and hold yourself empty for four seconds. Repeat this cycle twenty-one times.

After your premeditation, keep your eyes closed and maintain your relaxed position. Consciously take a slow, deep breath in and a slow, deep breath out. Take increasingly deeper, longer breaths in and deeper, longer breaths out. Slow down your breathing. Continue to do this, staying as still as your breathing will allow. Begin to do these meditation sessions for five minutes, increasing the duration every few days. Eventually, you'll be up to an hour or even longer! When I finish a meditation session, I feel as if someone has injected life and vitality into my soul. That renewed vigor and excitement gives me all the energy I need to complete my purpose, and I know it'll have a similar effect on you!

Every person I've introduced to meditation is now on the right path to becoming the best them they can be. Only in silence and reflection can you discover who you truly are and learn what you truly came into this world to accomplish.

Meditation is a game-changing, *world-changing* tool. I'm so grateful this amazing tool crossed my path, and you'll be grateful, too. I'm convinced if every person on the planet used meditating as a tool in their arsenal then the entire world would change for the better. I pray my book plays a part in the conscious evolution of humanity worldwide.

Journaling

The human mind is an incredible machine that we've barely tapped into as a society. If we don't write our thoughts down, they become lost forever. Inspiration can strike at any time and in any place. You should record your thoughts and ideas before you lose them. Journaling is the tool that creates a written record of your current perspective and gives a snapshot of your journey.

It's amazing to reflect on who you were in the past. By journaling, you'll be able to track your progress, remind yourself of things you may have forgotten, and rediscover past lessons learned. You'll be able to teach your loved ones and even reteach *yourself* things you may have overlooked.

In my opinion, journaling is one of the most underutilized practices in the self-development / awakening movement. But what better way to know your whole self than to read your own words?

I keep all of my journals. One of my favorite things to do at the end of each year or even from month the month is to reread my past journal entries.

When I look at my journal entries from years ago, I compare my goals from back then to where I am now. I ask myself, *What were some of my goals years ago? Did I achieve those goals, forget them, or have my goals changed drastically?*

Your journals can be very important for the outside world, but they're especially important for your personal journey. On one hand, you can change the world with your words! Keep track of them, because you never know whose life will be impacted by your written thoughts. On the other hand, journaling helps you always remember what you want out of life. Journaling helps to keep your desired path fresh in your mind.

Our day-to-day lives make it easy for us to get caught up and forget our passions. Journals help remind you of your desires. This is especially true if you keep a journal with you at all times and make a habit of writing in and reading it. Try to read your old journal entries periodically, whether it be once a year, every six months, or even monthly. Reread your journal however many times you need to in order to stay inspired, motivated, and on the transformative path to awakening the warrior within.

I've journaled in many different ways, but I have developed a very consistent method I've used for the past two and a half years.

Right after finishing my meditation and affirmations, I quickly proceed to journaling while my mind is still clear. I like to record my thoughts in the morning shortly after waking up because this is when my mind is at its freshest. And when my mind is fresh, the things I write will be fresh and not at all manipulated by outside forces.

Sometimes I like to write down my dreams. Other times I write about how I'm feeling in that moment. Then, I record 10 to 20 things I'm grateful for at that time. I try to write things I didn't have to spend money on, for example, a feeling, a state of mind, or even a relationship.

After recording a few things I'm thankful for, I write down the one thing I can do today that will move the needle for my life, business, relationship, or whatever I'm focused on at that time—the *one* thing. I make *one* thing my *only* priority. Having multiple priorities is unrealistic. Having many priorities will eventually cause you to neglect something. You need to focus on one thing and finish up with that thing before you move on to the next.

Of course it's great to have other tasks and ideas in your peripheral vision. Completing all of these things will move you towards your definite, chief aim, but your *main* focus should be on accomplishing that one priority.

Don't tell me you have a million things to do today because that's bullshit! I'm talking about finishing that one, important thing you've been avoiding because you're being a punk ass bitch and are scared of failure *or* success.

Keep your journal with you at all times. Read it all day long to remind yourself of your one, main priority of the day if you haven't already accomplished it. It takes a lot of discipline to do first things first, so until you do, use your journal as a constant reminder. Remember, there's nothing else that really should be done that day besides that *one* important thing. Use the power of journaling to help you take care of business!

Contemplation

Contemplation is a tool I discovered in a book about three and a half years ago. I don't remember the author of the book, but he or she advised readers to include contemplation in their morning routines. After journaling, write down a question or thought (in the form of a word, phrase, or complete sentence). Then, focus on it for five minutes.

Before this, I don't think I'd ever focused on just one thing for a full five minutes in my whole life! Like most people, I was always taught you had to

multitask in order to be productive. But as I said before, I've learned that multitasking is the enemy of all high-level productivity.

When I began to consciously evolve and awaken the warrior within, I implemented contemplation into my routine. I'd write a question or thought. Once I wrote something down, I'd sit in an empty room with absolutely no distractions. I'd turn off all communication and electronic devices. I made sure to use the restroom beforehand so even my own bladder wouldn't interrupt me! The only things I'd have with me were a cup of water, a pen, and a notepad. Then I'd sit and stare at what I'd written and write down anything and everything that came to mind about the question or thought of the day. I would push it!

Every week and a half, I'd add five to ten minutes to my contemplation. It was hard! I really had to grind the gears of my mind to not only focus on something for longer periods of time, but to also come up with in-depth answers and thoughts related to what I'd written.

I was forced to go deeper and deeper with my thoughts. You can't give one-word responses when you're tasked with thinking about a particular topic for twenty or thirty minutes! I'd really have to think about what the question or thought meant to me.

My responses to the daily topic became more detailed and interesting.

After recording the topic, I'd ask myself, *How I can implement this into my life? Why did I choose to write this today? What is the thought* behind *this thought [or question]? What could the author of this thought [or question] have been going through to say [or ask] this? What am I going through that made this resonate with me?*

I would sit for twenty or thirty minutes, sometimes more, trying to answer these questions. Doing so created an abundance of focus in my mind.

My newfound abundance of focus transferred into other areas of my life. My focus improved my jiu jitsu immediately because I was able to hone in on problems and solve them quickly without thinking of anything else. Contemplation helped my relationships by conditioning me to give my undivided attention. I began to focus on what people were actually saying to me without being distracted by texting or other preoccupations in my mind. Contemplation taught me to be present and in the moment.

No one told me about the awesome side effects of contemplation. I'd simply read about it in a book and had a friend say, "Hey, you should try this. It's going to be dope." I tried contemplation because I'm a curious man, even though some people who'd read the book I mentioned told me they didn't get anything out of it. I'm glad I decided to make up my own mind, because contemplation has changed my life.

There's gold beneath your feet *right now*. All you need are the tools and self-discipline to find it!

Once you start practicing silent contemplation and self-discipline, you'll find success, love, and an inner peace like never before. You will become the best version of yourself, and the warrior inside will be ready to strike.

Walk Your Truth (The Warrior Routine)

In order to walk your truth and live by the principles I present to you, you have to be diligent in eradicating the enemy within so that your warrior may thrive.

An old African proverb states, "When there is no enemy within, the enemy outside cannot hurt you." In order to rid yourself of the enemy within, you need to conquer your internal demons and use every resource available to you. This may seem easy, but fear, resistance, and a lack of discipline will

constantly try to revolt against your newfound warrior lifestyle.

You must awaken the lonely warrior who has been living inside you all these years and develop self-discipline. This is the only way to find true success.

Leonardo da Vinci said, "You will never have a greater or lesser dominion than that over yourself. The height of a man's success is gauged by his self-mastery; the depth of his failure by his self-abandonment."

The most simple yet challenging thing you will ever have do in life is consistently develop your self-mastery. Doing so will help you realize your definite, chief aim.

Things are going to come up. There will be distractions. Tragedy will almost surely strike at some point. There might be bankruptcies or foreclosures, fights, or setbacks around you. But you must stay focused on your definite, chief aim. Do not let the distractions get inside and disrupt your inner peace. Acknowledge the distractions. After all, they are happening to you and your family. But you must remember your goal and your purpose. Your purpose is the attainment of your higher self. Your purpose is to awaken the warrior within. Never let distractions make you lose sight of this.

Though it is very simple, the Warrior Routine is not easy. There are many stages of the Warrior Routine, and now I'll teach you the first one. The first stage is the easiest stage of the entire Warrior Routine, but many see it as the hardest because it is the start of something new. It's usually difficult to go from doing nothing to doing something!

The blue belt is the belt with the most meaning in Brazilian jiu jitsu. It is the first belt after the white belt, and it signifies that you've come to know something. Knowing *something* is the biggest jump you can take from knowing *nothing*. Coming to know something about yourself through this Warrior Routine is one of the biggest leaps you will ever take. It can be the easiest leap, or it can be the hardest. It all depends on your mindset and level of commitment.

The Warrior Routine, Step-by-Step

When you wake up, don't check any messages. I personally don't have a cell phone anymore so I never have to check one. Don't check your computer. Don't speak to anyone. As soon as you wake up, brush your teeth, then drink two cups of warm lemon water. After your water, sit down and immediately get started with at least five minutes of silent meditation.

You'll probably have to wake up a little earlier than you do presently. The Warrior Routine must begin first thing every morning. Starting early every morning will positively change the outcome of your entire day. So get up, brush your teeth, drink your water, then sit down and focus on your breathing for at least five minutes of silent meditation.

After your meditation, you'll recite the affirmations, or Warrior Code, I've outlined in this book. I suggest you start with one of the codes and recite it one hundred times on your first day. On the second day, pick two of the codes. You can recite each one fifty times, or recite both codes one hundred times each (this is what I recommend). The more you repeat these codes, the more passion you put behind reciting them, the better. Feel the truth and depth of the Warrior Code. Become one with what you're saying. Don't simply recite the Warrior Code, live it.

When you're done with your affirmations, begin journaling. Write how you feel, or record one of your dreams. Then, write five to ten things you're grateful for in that moment. That's it for journaling. Be sure to write the date on your journal entry, then move on to five minutes of contemplation. After completing your meditation, affirmations, journaling, and contemplation exercises, move on to five to thirty minutes of medium to high intensity physical exercise.

As a warrior, this is how you should begin each day. Once you've completed the Warrior Routine, you can officially start your day.

Chapter 1.1: Choose Consciously

"I'm committed to consciously choosing the activities I pursue."

I know I can do anything. However, I can't do *everything*. I am in charge of what I do and who I spend time with, and you should be, too. A lot of opportunities and interesting people will come into your life as you progress and awaken the warrior within. It's up to you to choose the people and opportunities that align with your purpose.

Along with the many new people you'll meet, a lot of people from your past will come back into your life. More and more people will be attracted to your newfound wisdom, peace, energy, and love of life, and they'll want to spend time or do business with you. Some of these people and opportunities will be good for you; others, you should avoid. For this reason, you have to, have to, *have to* learn how to say no as a full sentence. "No." Period.

If someone invites you to an activity unrelated to your definite, chief aim or life's purpose, the answer is no. If you're making money and working towards your goals and someone invites you to go out drinking, the answer is no. If something work-related comes up during quality time you'd promised to your family, the answer is no!

When you're on your deathbed, you won't remember everything you did. You *will* remember the things you regret *not* doing—the chances you didn't take, the commitments you didn't keep, the dreams you didn't pursue. You'll remember the time you wasted, the promises you broke, and the people you neglected. It's up to you to minimize your regrets and live your best life each day.

It's very important for you to consciously choose how to spend your time. We all have a limited amount of time here on Earth. We have to be careful with our investments of such a limited resource. Devoting time is making a valuable investment. When you spend time on something, you're making an investment in a person, an idea, or a belief system.

Invest wisely. Allocate time to the things that mean most to you. If health is important to you, invest time in going to the gym and preparing nutritious meals. If your family's important to you, invest time in hanging out with them and doing fun activities. If your relationship with your spouse is important to you, spend one-on-one time and have date nights. If your relationship with God is important to you, allot time to prayer and meditation. If making money is a top priority for you, then get on your grind!

Do the things you have to *and* want to do. Resist being a yes-man or yes-woman for fear of criticism. Say no to things you know you shouldn't do. Say no to the things you don't want to do. Your productivity and life will be so much better if you simply learn to say no!

Remember, you can do anything but not *everything*. You don't have time to do everything this world has to offer. Choose carefully and focus on what's most important to you.

Chapter 1.2: Invest Wisely

"I am here to lead a glorious life and to be the hero of my story. I will only use my time in ways that benefit my growth or the growth of others. I will not mindlessly drift or indulge in activities that do not improve my capacity as a well-rounded, peaceful person, because my time on this planet is limited."

How you invest your time is the most important investment of your entire existence. We all start each day with the same 24 hours ahead of us. The proverbial playing field is level for us all. Each of us has 86,400 seconds every day. We all have 86,400 opportunities for self-growth and self-realization.

I used to spend about two hours a day watching TV. Two hours per day never really seemed like a big deal. It was just two measly hours out of twenty-four! What else could I possibly do in two hours? One day, instead of watching tv, I started reading a book on time management.

The book advised me to write down everything I did throughout the day and how much time I devoted to each activity. I was to do this for a whole week. Recording for a week was hard and took a lot of discipline. It actually took me about three weeks to get it right because I kept forgetting about the task. But when I finally got it right, the results were daunting.

So my two hours of TV a day turned into 14 hours of tv per week, right? Well 14 hours a week is 728 hours a year! 728 hours is the equivalent of 30 ⅓ days. To make things simple, let's say I spend 12 hours per day awake and 12 hours sleeping. Factoring in sleeping time, I spent the equivalent of 60 ⅔ days per year watching TV. That's over two months of TV!

I used to spend *at least* three hours a day on my phone texting, making calls, checking emails, browsing the web, and playing games. Those 21

hours per week became 1,092 hours per year, the equivalent of 45 ½ non-stop days or 91 days per year when factoring in sleeping. Whoa! 91 days spent on my phone!

As soon as I saw the big picture and understood how much time I was wasting on trivial tasks, I got rid of my TV. We no longer have a TV in our home. Then, I worked on getting rid of my cellphone. I've been without a cellphone for over two years now. These are just some of the things I cut out of my life to become focused on self-mastery and awakening the warrior within, and my productivity and levels of consciousness have never been better.

Think about it: In what activities do you mindlessly indulge? If you can't think of anything, find out! Take a tally of everything you do for just one day. Record everything exactly, e.g. the time you wake up, time allocated for checking social media, time spent in the bathroom, etc. After successfully tallying your day, think about the things you did that were a complete waste of time. My guess is you squandered big chunks of time on tasks that have nothing to do with your purpose or your loved ones. Think about the activities you can get rid of to spend more time reading, taking classes, exercising, preparing healthy meals, catching up with a friend, or hanging out with your family.

Self-discipline and mastery of time are necessities when it comes to awakening your warrior. Remember: You are here to lead a glorious life and to be the hero of your own story. Use your time only in ways that benefit your growth or the growth of others. Our time on this planet is limited. Don't carelessly partake in activities that weaken your warrior spirit.

Chapter 2: Feed Your Mind

"I will personally choose only the best thoughts to feed my mind."

You must be cognizant of what you feed your mind. Doing so will change the way you receive and process information. If you change the way you process information, you'll change the way you think. Changing what you think will change what you say. And by changing what you say, you'll change what you *do*. So how can the simple statement, "I will personally choose only the best thoughts to feed my mind" change your life so thoroughly?

Personally choosing the thoughts you allow in your mind makes you "the master of your fate, and the captain of your soul" as in William Ernest Henley's "Invictus." You'll become selective of the thoughts you allow to take root in your mind, the people you surround yourself with, and the activities you participate in.

Since I decided to personally choose the best thoughts for myself, I stopped watching television. I also stopped listening to the radio and cut out any overly-aggressive music or music that didn't make me feel good. As you evolve, your taste in music will evolve. The music I grew up with, music about people killing each other, selling drugs, and degrading women stopped making me feel good. Music about love, life, and nature began to make me feel good because that's what I wanted more of in my life.

As I evolved, I wanted more peace and harmony in my life. I grew up in a very hostile, relatively dangerous environment. My friends and I roamed the streets day and night. We sold drugs and got into fights. Some of my friends have been shot and killed. I've had friends overdose on drugs. A few of my friends are in prison for murder. I could've been like many of my old friends, but I wanted more from life. Just as I had to choose, you also have the responsibility and duty to choose the thoughts you accept into your mind. What are we if we're not our thoughts? Thoughts create words, and words create deeds. So if you don't carefully choose your thoughts, you might look up and find yourself somewhere you don't want to be. Have you been choosing your thoughts, words, and actions carefully? Are you happy with where you are or with what you've done up until this point? If not, it's time to start choosing more carefully.

I don't mean for you to choose carefully in a cautious, scared sense. I mean I want you to choose thoughts, words, and actions that align with your major purpose in life and your duty to this planet. Personally choosing the best thoughts to feed your mind will affect your being at the deepest level. Your thoughts will permeate and become the truest essence of who you are. Following this code will trigger the best parts of you. It will trigger the most decisive parts of you; the parts that don't care about the criticism of others. Following this code will trigger the parts of you that awaken the warrior within.

Chapter 3: Take Responsibility for Your Life

"I will never blame, complain about, or criticize anyone for their thoughts, deeds, or actions. I live my life with full responsibility for all that happens to me."

I blamed others for my failures and regrets in life for a long time. I got in trouble with the law? It was the cops' fault. I wasn't doing so well in school? It was because the professors didn't really care about us and wanted us to fail so we'd have to repeat their courses and pay them more money. I lost a student at my gym? It was the former student's fault for being an asshole and canceling his or her membership. Tardy for an appointment? It was the train's fault for coming an hour late. Didn't land a client? It was because the potential client was a dick and I was glad he decided not to use my services. I used to complain that my friends were assholes. I used to complain that all the girls who didn't want me were sluts. Man, I used to dish out blame to

everything and everyone! I didn't realize how responsible I was for my own life.

I used to criticize the government, business owners, celebrities, politicians, my friends, women I dated, classmates, teachers—the list goes on and on, and on, and on.

I was a part of the walking dead. If playing the blame game sounds like something you do, you need to slap yourself awake right now! Repeat after me: I will never blame, complain about, or criticize anyone for their thoughts, deeds, or actions. I live my life with full responsibility for all that happens to me.

One way or another, you're responsible for everything that happens to you. You're responsible for reaping what you've sown in the past. You're also responsible for dealing with, stepping away from, and moving on from what someone else has done to you. It is not your duty to blame, complain, or criticize. No matter what, your duty is to live your purpose. Don't let anyone or anything ever let you forget that.

I posted a sign in my house that reads, *There is no blaming, there is no complaining, and there is no criticizing in this household. This is a positive household. Please help to keep it that way*. This sign helps me and everyone around me take responsibility for our lives.

Of course there will be times when we experience injustices. Things you don't like will surely happen. Loved ones will die. Someone may steal from or violate you. I understand these things happen. I get it. You aren't responsible for the actions of others, but you *are* responsible for your *reactions*. Acknowledge the bad stuff and move on. You and you alone are responsible for your mental, physical, emotional, and spiritual health. Complaining, blaming, and criticizing will only take away from your overall health and destroy you from the inside. You are responsible for your peace. Find a way to maintain it.

Man up! Woman up! Stop fucking complaining, blaming, and criticizing others for what they do. Their actions have nothing to do with you. Work on yourself. If you can change yourself, you can change the whole world. Change yourself, and the world will open up to reveal the magic that can be found all around you.

Chapter 4: Learn Forever

"I will make a daily commitment to continuously and consistently search for ways to learn, implement, and evolve strategies to become a more formidable warrior in every aspect of my life."

I've met many different types of people and been in many social circles throughout my life. I've been friends with drug dealers, entrepreneurs, members of the spirituality community, athletes, doctors, nurses, lawyers, accountants and so many others who fall in between or on the outskirts of these professions. Though these people have many different paths, they all seem to be missing the same major pieces to life's puzzle, and most of them have trouble admitting it.

Entrepreneurs sacrifice relationships, health, leisure, spirituality, and oftentimes their purpose for the love of money. The spirituality community is always complaining about being broke, and many of them are surprisingly unhealthy. Besides the small number of professionals, most athletes are typically broke.

And though most athletes are enjoying themselves and following their perceived purpose, many of them sacrifice their health and relationships.

People with specialized, professional careers, such as doctors, nurses, lawyers, and accountants, make good money. Or at least they *think* they're making good money. However, a lot of them are sacrificing their health and happiness in order to make that money.

Life is made of a lot of different parts. It's important for you to take time to develop the significant aspects of your life. The happiest people know that the key to a good life is forging good relationships. Tend to the relationships in your life—this includes your relationship with yourself, your loved ones, business partners, your environment, etc.—to be happy, healthy, and successful. If your relationships aren't secure, start getting yourself together!

Get your finances in order. Start making more money by providing more value. Think of ways to turn your hobbies or passions into profitable business endeavors!

Take care of yourself. Consider your health. Eat great food; organic, non-GMO, and local. Include more plant-based meals in your recipes. Exercise every day and don't be weak! A sorry 30-minute walk three times a week is not going to cut it! Get strong. Take care of your body.

Develop a relationship with the universe, with God, with the divine. Enjoy the benefits of peace and spirituality in your life. Growing up, I personally never had a relationship with God or the universe. I was pretty much an Atheist, even though my mom and grandmother were Christian, my dad is Jewish, and most of my friends were Roman Catholic. These past few years have brought me closer to God. That newfound relationship has immensely improved my life and guided me through my darkest days.

Do the things you love. Have fun! Be spontaneous. Travel. Don't live in fear. Be adventurous! Take yourself to the next level and keep evolving.

Find your purpose then chase it. Chase it. Never stop chasing it! Everything you take in, everything you learn, everything you do, and every positive change you implement will take you to the next level, help you evolve, and made you a stronger warrior. What are you waiting for? Your happiness and success await!

Chapter 5: Recharge To Serve

"I cannot give what I don't have. So I will practice daily self-care because I know the only way to help others is to first help myself."

I have a question for you: How can you give something you don't have? How can you help others change their lives if your life is in shambles? How can you help others be healthy if you have one foot in the grave? How can you help others be free if you're still enslaved? How can you help others make more money if you're still broke? In short, you can't!

Growing up, I was always told selfishness was a bad, shameful character trait. I wouldn't make many friends being selfish. I had to be selfless and giving. But I was also told not to give *too* much, for fear of being taken advantage of. That was so weird and confusing for me as a child! Share, but don't share *too* much. Love, but don't love *too* much. The phrase "too much" was always attached to everything I learned about being selfless and helping others.

The whole problem with this type of selflessness and giving is that it's built on fear and not based on love.

With this brand of selflessness instilled in me, with that foundational belief system, I had many trials and tribulations. I often found myself giving too much. But who really knows how much is too much until you've given it, right? So I had to stop and regroup my life and my views. I researched, discovered, and implemented how to take care of myself. The first thing I had to do was stop trying to pull others along with me before I was strong enough to pull them. I had to take care of myself first.

I realized the only way to be truly selfless is to first be selfish. You can't help others if you still need help yourself. Jim Rohn once said, "The greatest gift you can give somebody is your own personal development. I used to say, 'If you will take care of me, I will take care of you.' Now I say, 'I will take care of me for you, if you will take care of you for me.'"

You've probably heard the oxygen mask example, but let's reiterate it here. If an airplane is going down, put an oxygen mask on yourself first. Why? Well, if you help someone else before you help yourself, how do you know they'll be able to help you? How can you ensure you'll still be in good enough condition to help yourself after helping others? You don't know these things for sure. But if you put the oxygen mask on yourself first, you'll be able to help the whole plane.

Through self-care and practicing the Warrior Routine, you'll build a solid foundation to inspire others to improve their lives as well. With your strengthened beliefs and successes, you'll be in a position to really give your time, energy, and resources to others.

Remember, the only way you can give is if you first *have*. So it's important to create a good life and have what you need before you give freely to others. As Eleanor Brownn once said, "Self-care is not selfish. You cannot serve from an empty vessel." Get yourself together first. Then, go change the world!

Chapter 5.1: Feed Your Soul

"As silence is the best spiritual investment for the soul, I will feed my soul silence everyday."

We've already discussed the amazing results and benefits of stepping into the void with daily meditation. Millions of people around the world attest to the healing powers of meditation, myself included. Feeding my soul silence through meditation is one of the most crucial foundational blocks of my life. This code is non-negotiable for me, as I truly know what silence and meditation can do. Silence is the best spiritual investment. I feel a profound inner peace everyday after feeding myself silence. I become re-energized and recommitted to deal with whatever comes my way. Silence prepares my soul for the world like nothing else can!

The silent void is my favorite place to be. In silence, I rediscover who I am. Once I committed to daily silence and meditation, things began to shift. I felt a newfound sense of peace, and my relationships with myself, my environment, and my loved ones greatly improved. My daily devotion to silence and feeding my soul helped me to grow closer to my family and friends. I stopped screaming at my kids. I stopped arguing with my wife. These changes weren't instantaneous, of course. They happened gradually through my daily practice of meditation, through my love of silence and stepping into the void, through my love of life. I can't stress enough how full your soul will feel if you feed it a little silence everyday.

Silence kept me balanced when I lived in New York City. That same silence still helps me improve, grow, and evolve through a conscious effort to awaken the warrior within me. Every single day, I sit in silence and go deeper and deeper to awaken the warrior, and you can, too. There's a warrior in all of us. Feed your soul silence to awaken the warrior residing in you!

Chapter 6: Focus

"I will only do one task at a time to achieve my goals. I know that multitasking is the enemy of high-level productivity and a symptom of resistance."

I was always taught that multitasking was the way to get things done. I used to be proud of how well I multitasked! I could drive while eating and texting. I could hold a conversation while texting or writing an email. Basically, I could do anything I wanted to do while doing something else.

The problem was, I wasn't getting anything done *well*. If I ate and texted while I drove, then I drove like shit, my texts were barely coherent, and I usually spilled some food. If I tried to hold a conversation while texting or emailing, I'm sure the other person felt jilted because the only thing present in my in-person conversations was my body. My life basically sucked because I kept trying to do everything at once. In turn, I was either getting nothing done, or doing everything poorly. Every task or goal would get about 10% of my effort. I was nowhere near doing my best work.

Life changes when you get things done at 100%. When you finally pare down and focus on finishing one thing at a time before beginning another, your life will change. When you type "The End" on that book you've been working on forever, your life will change. When you finish a course, your life will change. When you sit down and give your full attention to someone who values your opinion, your life (and that relationship) will change!

When I realized I was just giving 10% effort to everything in my life, it shocked and scared the shit out of me. I used to identify with results instead of identifying with the journey. I didn't think of all I'd learned on the way to achieving a goal, I just wanted to check another thing off my list. It didn't matter if I didn't give my best. Trying to do so many things at once kept me from being focused on my life's purpose. I was running around, doing everything half-assed, getting nowhere.

Through soul-searching, I soon realized why I operated that way. Besides multitasking being heralded as a good thing most of my life, I knew I was scared of failure *and* of success. I knew that if I focused on one thing, whether it be a relationship, project, or idea, then I was all in. And if I was all in and that one thing failed, then *I* was a failure. If it was a success, I'd be burdened with *always* being a success. I was hedging my bets by doing a lot of stuff at once.

Multitasking is an activity built upon fear. Once I decided to stop multitasking, I *really* started to achieve my goals. And I did more than simply check something off a list, I lived in the moment and did everything to my best ability. Whether I was building my first successful company, building my *second* successful company, hiring employees to outsource and delegate my tasks, coming up with a new product, or even writing this book, I completed each task one-by-one and with zest and renewed focus.

Man, there are a million things I could have been doing while writing this book! But I cleared my schedule and made sure this was the only thing I'd be working on. As I've abandoned multitasking, I wasn't going to tackle any other projects. I'd just write this book. And honestly, deciding not to multitask is the only reason this book actually got completed!

Multitasking is a way for us to run away from ourselves and our relationships. It's a tool for you to resist giving your whole self to something. I've been on an evolutionary journey ever since I stopped multitasking. You should stop multitasking, too. I promise it'll change your life and get you one step closer to fully awakening your warrior.

Chapter 7: Win-Win

"I will only engage in transactions that benefit all of whom they affect."

Growing up in Brooklyn in a culture of drugs and violent crime, almost everything we did was win-lose. I mean, that's how TV told us to do business, that's how everyone I knew I did business. In order for someone to win, another person had to lose.

I grew up in a very competitive environment. There had to be clear-cut winners and clear-cut losers. For example, for every person who made money from selling drugs, another person lost money and became addicted to harmful substances. In cases that weren't so clear-cut, winners and losers were typically decided through fights.

As I grew older, I abandoned a lot of those street values. Honesty and integrity became more and more important to me. And if you claim to have honesty and integrity, you can't run a win-lose business. Your aim should be a win-win or win-win-win business. Win-win would be good business to a consumer. Win-win-win would be a partnership with the consumer, or something along those lines.

I've been around many circles in which people put out products just to make money. Making money is cool, and I have nothing against it. But when it's at the expense of quality and to the disadvantage of consumers, I do have a problem. You shouldn't just try to make money because you're a great marketer and can sell to anyone. You shouldn't sell something knowing customers won't get their desired results, especially knowing most customers don't have money to frivolously spend. I have an issue with people who don't sell with integrity and honesty!

If we all interacted and did business with hopes of benefitting everyone involved, the world would be a much better place. The win-win ripple effect would start to permeate throughout the land. Child labor would disappear. People wouldn't be losing limbs to mine diamonds from villages. Shitty products would disappear! Even buyer's remorse would disappear because customers would no longer put their hearts and souls into crappy products and services.

We are all one. Imagine how much greater the environment would be if everyone did win-win transactions. As the win-lose businesses of the past are taking their toll on our oceans, forests, and wildlife, more and more people are finding environmentally healthy, stable ways to do business. This is especially important because if the environment loses, we all lose in the end. It's imperative we all adopt a win-win attitude now!

You should adopt a win-win model in every aspect of your life, not simply in business transactions. Adopt the win-win attitude in your personal relationship transactions as well. Relationships are transactions of energy, love, and support. Make an effort to engage in transactions that benefit everyone in all parts of your life. You'll improve your business and how you make money. You'll also improve your relationships with your family and friends, strangers, your environment, God, and with yourself.

How you do something is how you'll do everything. People don't compartmentalize behavior. You can't be honest and full of integrity in one aspect of your life and a fucking liar in another. It just doesn't work that way! I've never met someone who was honest, just, and good in one part of life while being a disgusting creep who rapes, mutilates, and steals in another part of their life. Whether we know it or not, our mentality and behavior carries on across the board. And good or bad, we implant those seeds into our subconscious every day. Furthermore, your behavior and actions towards others will eventually pay their dividends. We always reap what we sow. So be careful in all of your transactions. Choose carefully all of your words and promises. Choose carefully all of your deeds.

Only engage in transactions that benefit all of whom they affect. That, my friends, is how you awaken the warrior within. And when your thoughts, words, and deeds are aligned with truth and integrity, the warrior within becomes the warrior outside.

Chapter 8: The Secret to Success

"I will always make it a habit to deliver more than I am paid for because I know this is the fastest way to achieve my goals."

When I still had a gym and was coaching and teaching jiu jitsu, I essentially gave private lessons to the whole class. I'd go from student to student, giving individualized attention and answering each student's specific questions. Then, at the end of each class, I'd devote an extra ten to fifteen minutes to opening up the floor and addressing issues or additional questions. I did all of this because I wanted to create confident, competent jiu jitsu students.

Now, did I have to give personalized attention and spend extra time answering questions? No. Was I paid extra to do so? No. But I truly believe delivering more than I'm paid for is the fastest way to achieve my goals. Going the extra mile helped my students get better, faster. It also fostered a good relationship between me and my students, and increased my retention rate.

I offered and gave away free classes. At a certain point, I even started offering a free month of classes, which was very intense for me! And it didn't matter if a student had paid or was taking advantage of a free offer. My team and I always over-delivered to show people what we were really about. And I typically wanted to show people what I was about before they paid me, so I frequently gave samples of what I had to offer through my interactions and guidance.

When people *did* pay me, I was sure to over-deliver. If I promised something by Friday, I had it done by Wednesday. If I promised a 1% improvement, I improved by 10%. If I promised I'd change someone's life by 10%, I made sure to change it by 100%!

I always over-deliver because that's what I want to be known for. I want to build a legacy of going the extra mile, doing the hard stuff, and exceeding expectations. I always want to be the guy who's known for giving more than what's required. I over-deliver in my relationships, sex, on projects, teaching, in love, and with listening. Over-delivering has paid dividends for me in more ways than one every single day.

The more seeds you plant, the more things will grow, and the more you will have to harvest. What you reap, you will sow. By over-delivering, you'll be in charge of some very amazing things that will bear some very beautiful fruits for you. Your going above and beyond will manifest itself in the form of healthy relationships and financial security. So, over-deliver with your friends and family. Over-deliver on your job and in your business. Over-deliver in everything you do! If you do, I promise: The world will deliver everything you've ever dreamed of and more.

Chapter 9: Be Present

"I will be present and aware at all times and during every interaction because I know every moment is an opportunity to evolve myself and change the minds of others. I will listen at least *twice more than I speak."*

Evolving your consciousness is your birthright *and* your duty. You have 86,400 seconds to evolve and learn something new each day. You need to take advantage of every given opportunity by being present and aware.

As your consciousness and awareness expand, a lot of opportunities will present themselves to you. You're going to have opportunities like you've never had before. While evolution of consciousness will come through self-reflection, stepping into the void, reading, and journaling, a lot of your evolution will come through your interactions with others.

Be present during every moment and listen deeply to everything someone is telling you. Accept the lessons and energy offered by people you respect. Your consciousness will evolve and your life will radiate positive change again and again and again.

Of course, this doesn't mean for you to talk to every person you see. But as long as you're on the right path, the right people will present themselves to you. You'll feel an attraction urging you to speak with people throughout your day. You may be drawn to someone in line at the bank or post office, a friend of a friend, or even your waitress at a restaurant. People are here to show us either what to do, or what not to do. Open yourself up to the ideas, beliefs, and lessons waiting for you.

As I tell my son and all my students, God gave you two ears and one mouth for you to listen at least twice as much as you speak. Listening has become a forgotten art in our society, but it's necessary in each and every one of our relationships.

Listening, not speaking, is the key to being a master salesman. Sure, you can use your words to manipulate your potential customer into buying something. But when customers have been manipulated instead of having their needs met, they'll have buyer's remorse, a bad feeling in their stomachs, and will never trust you again. Listening is the key to salesmanship. Listening is the key to evolution.

So how can we recover the art of listening? We have to practice it consciously and daily! We must affirm to ourselves, "I will be present and aware at all times and during every interaction because I know every moment is an opportunity to evolve myself and change the minds of others. I will listen at least twice more than I speak." By simply hearing and internalizing just one new idea, with your determination to listen more driving you forward, your entire existence can change.

For example, when I heard about people selling products online, that one idea changed my life. Once I heard about online sales, internalized the idea in my mind, and implemented those ideas, the entire trajectory of my life changed! Hell, I probably wouldn't have written this book if I hadn't first heard thoughts and ideas from others about jiu jitsu, or dropping out of college, or becoming an author. Every lesson or idea given to me from people I respect has changed my course for the better in some way. Listen to what others are working on. Listen to what they think. You'll be inspired and determined to try something new.

Listening is one of the most important, if not *the* most important, skills you can master. Listening to others is key, but so is listening to yourself. We'll get to that a bit later.

The thing is, when you listen to someone, you not only help yourself become better, you help the person confiding in you become better. You invest your time, interest, and energy into hearing what they have to say, which lets them know they matter. People will be inspired to make sure they really say what they mean, because they know someone's listening. Most of us have to talk to people while they're texting, eating, or otherwise preoccupied. You should make a point to stand out as someone who really gives a damn about what people have to say. Remember, stop the multitasking. When people speak to you, focus solely on them and their words. You never know, they just might say something your warrior within has been waiting to hear.

Chapter 10: Build Your Character

"I am committed to keeping promises to myself and others because I know this is the best way to build and increase self-confidence."

I used to get sick a lot when I was younger. On those days when I was sick in bed, I enjoyed playing video games. I really liked games with the "build your own character" option; I loved building my character any way I wanted. I picked his clothes, his character traits, and his physical attributes. Creating a character who looked like me or who looked how I wanted to look really helped make those sick days bearable.

Reflecting on those days, I realized life is a lot like those video games I used to play. We're all characters, and many of us get lost in the game and never *change* our characters. But as you awaken the warrior within, you'll realize that while you may be a character in the game of life, you also are a player who has control. You have the ability to change your character and make it whatever you want it to be.

When I started to see life as one big video game, I knew I had the power to change and rebuild my character in any way I saw fit. I could alter my character traits and become a better player in the game. One of the first alterations I decided to make was to give my character more self-confidence.

I soon understood that the best way for me to have more self-confidence was to keep promises to myself and others. When I keep promises to myself, I hold myself accountable and become more and more sure of my ability to deliver. When I keep my promises to others, I establish myself as a trustworthy, dependable person. My self-confidence soars because not only am I getting what I want and helping others, my desired image is being seen by the rest of the world. Keep your promises. You'll be amazed at what it does for your confidence!

Chapter 10.1: Six Levels of Truth

"I will maintain honesty and integrity in my thoughts, words, and actions."

In my experience, there are what I like to call the Six Levels of Truth. The first and lowest level is not lying in your actions. This means you don't steal, rob, rape, kill, or cheat.

The second level is not lying in your words. This obviously means speaking the truth. Do you know people who are always honest with their words? People who refuse to tell even "white" lies? Do you know someone who would rather remain silent than tell a lie? If so, these people are on Level Two.

Level Three is not lying in your thoughts. This level is a bit more personal and private. To illustrate this level, think about when you tell yourself you're going to do something. Do you *actually* think you're going to do it? Do you think you'll *actually* commit? If you can't honestly and wholeheartedly say yes, you're lying in your thoughts.

How much do you lie to yourself? How often do you rationalize things that aren't good for you? You might find yourself saying stuff like, "Eating this one donut will be okay." Or, "It's fine to cheat sometimes," or, "I don't really like alcohol but it's okay to drink sometimes," or, "I think smoking is bad but it's okay to smoke sometimes." If you find yourself saying stuff like this, you aren't on Level Three. Not lying in your thoughts means not rationalizing stupid shit.

Level Four is truth in your actions. It's when you go out of your way to commit honest acts. It's returning a wallet no matter how much money is inside it. It's giving a cashier money back when he or she gives you too much change. It's finding and returning a brand new smartphone even though you're stuck with a raggedy flip phone. Level Four is living according to your higher self, and possessing integrity and truth even when you can get away with dishonest actions.

Let me point out that "not lying" isn't exactly the same as "truth." "Not lying" is when you do the bare minimum to stay honest. You may not steal, but you might keep a wallet if you find one. You might not speak lies, but you also hold back your true thoughts. You might know what's best for everyone, but you rationalize bad behavior to let yourself and others off the hook. "Truth" is when you're being your most honest, highest self.

Level Five is truth in your words. How many people do you know who always tell the truth? I'm not talking about people who simply don't lie. I mean

people who tell the truth no matter what. They don't hold back and will say what needs to be said. These people are transparent in their professional and personal lives.

Having truth in your words doesn't mean you don't keep private matters private. You don't have to tell everyone everything. But it does mean being honest about the things you keep to yourself. If someone asks about something they aren't ready to discuss, people on level five might say, "I can't talk to you about that right now because I'm keeping it to myself." That's truth in words.

As you may have guessed, Level Six is truth in thoughts. Being on this level means you never rationalize dishonest or harmful things. When you have truth in your thoughts, you stay aligned with who you are and what you believe. It is at this level you become your truest self. You tell yourself how it is and constantly self-reflect. You hold yourself accountable and regularly remind yourself of your purpose. The warrior within is truly awakened at this level.

As an example, if you tell yourself you won't eat anymore fried foods, then find yourself at a table with someone's order of French fries, remember your commitment to truth in thoughts. Look at those fries and tell yourself you already have a pre-existing decision. You're honest and have integrity, so you

won't even think of eating one of those fries, no matter what anyone says or does. It doesn't matter if everyone else is eating like shit. You said you'd only eat the healthiest, best quality food. Those French fries aren't worth disappointing yourself and all six levels of truth.

Staying on Level Six definitely takes work. It's not always going to be easy, but you must persevere. You might not know many Level Six people yet, but once you get there yourself, others with truth in thoughts will be attracted to you. You'll meet people and be able to tell from their words and actions if they're anywhere near having truth in their thoughts. As you become the warrior you're destined to be, you'll recognize the warrior in others.

Once you have reached Level Six and have truth in your thoughts, you'll know your mission is to create more warriors. I know my mission is to help awaken the warrior within you so that you can then do the same for someone else. Through the warrior-awakening ripple effect, people's lives will vastly improve. More and more people will be their best, most productive selves, and will live their highest truth with integrity. The world will truly be a better place.

Chapter 11: Awaken the Warrior Within

"If there is ever a misunderstanding, I will courageously speak my truth. I know angry thoughts left to fester in the mind grow wings, tails, and teeth in no time."

How many of your relationships have been ruined because of a small misunderstanding growing into a huge juggernaut? You have probably no idea. I never really considered how many relationships I'd ruined because I let a seed of misunderstanding turn into an angry thought, which then turned into an angry word, that in turn festered into an angry deed. Those minor misunderstandings quickly grew into giant monsters that consumed both of our egos and destroyed everything in their paths.

I thought I was always right, and anyone who didn't agree with me was always wrong. Does this sound like you? I bet it does.

When I say everything in the wake of a misunderstanding can be destroyed, I mean *everything*. It isn't just one relationship that's affected. Your relationship with one person defines your relationship with everyone.

So, the angrier you become in one relationship, the more it boils over into your other relationships. For this reason, it's very important to clear up misunderstandings. Not just for the sake of saving that one relationship with one person, but for every other relationship in your live, including your relationships with yourself.

Anything left to fester in the mind very, *very* quickly grows into a monster. This is especially true if you have a support system of yes-men and yes-women. These people don't have your best interest at heart, and they'll agree with everything you say. If you say a guy is an asshole, a yes-man will say, "You're right! He *is* an asshole!" These people love drama, complaining, and blaming. They will never try to calm you down or offer a different, more rational perspective. Yes-men and yes-women make it harder for you to courageously speak your truth and squash disagreements. If you truly value your relationships, get rid of yes-men and yes-women right away.

Awaken the warrior inside. Step into your courage, speak your truth, and mend the valuable relationships in your life. Respectfully clear up the misunderstandings, address the pain with love, and continue on your awesome, inspirational path.

Chapter 12: Be a Warrior!

"I will do the things, say the words, and think the thoughts of a warrior, even in the face of adversity and criticism. I know my growth will eventually inspire even my worst critics to be the best they can be."

Criticism is one of our biggest fears. It was surely my biggest personal barrier before achieving success. Not only was I afraid of failure, I was afraid of what others would think of me *after* a failure. I was afraid of being called a loser or hearing people call me crazy. I was afraid of hearing, "I told you so." My ego just couldn't take it!

I was even more afraid of success! I was scared to be in the spotlight. I didn't want people thinking I just got lucky. People might say I didn't deserve my success, and I might be labeled a fraud. They might say, "He's a fake! He's a phony!" Again, my ego couldn't take it.

But as I continued to walk my truth and awaken the warrior living inside me, I realized everyone's a critic!

Other people's criticisms are just opportunities to reaffirm my inner peace, courage, and strength, and to stay true in my thoughts, words, and deeds. I used the critics to become more in tune with my higher self and my purpose.

Critics always play small, and criticisms never come from a place of love; criticism comes from fear. Critics never step into the arena to take the necessary blow to win a battle. Critics love the safety of the sidelines. Critics usually aren't bad people, they've simply given in to the fear society says we all should feel.

Surprisingly (or maybe not), your biggest critics will always be those closest to you. You'll begin to make others uncomfortable as you awaken your warrior. Your growth and improvements will show that your critics are not living in *their* truth. So instead of finding out who they really are and making changes of their own, people will start to criticize you. After all, it's much easier to try to dim someone else's light than to figure out how to shine your own.

I was always told not to aspire to be rich, because rich people are bad. I was told not to aim for the spotlight, because then you'll be talked about. Fear of criticism was ingrained in me at a very young age.

As a child, if I ever went against cultural norms, some would ask, "What are people going to say about you?" When I wanted to wear something different from everyone else, I heard, "What will people think?" I used to be terrified of standing out and being different. I used to let the critics win.

I've since learned that the longer you walk in your truth and live the life you're designed to live, the more your critics will become your fans. Eventually, criticism all but disappears.

Continue to walk in your truth. Work on self-mastery, and leave proverbial bread crumbs for the critics. Don't judge them or say "I told you so" when they start to follow your lead. Simply smile and love them unconditionally.

I've never really been into the Bible, but it has some pretty amazing quotes in it. I hope you devout Bible readers will excuse my butchering of this quote, but Jesus said something like, "It's very easy to love those who love you, but your reward will be great if you learn to love those that are your enemies." Remember: Live your truth, go after your purpose, and love everyone. Live the life of a warrior!

Final Thoughts

The Warrior Routine is life-changing. When I achieved self-mastery and discipline, the warrior within me truly awakened and evolved. I began to think clearly, my path became more apparent, and I held my definite, chief aim within my grasp. If you follow the Warrior Routine, you'll experience amazing changes, too. You may need additional guidance as you continue on your warrior's journey. Use the following chapters to help you stay encouraged. Be strong, work hard, and let the warrior within you thrive!

Abandon Your Fears and Quiet Critics

"I will walk my truth and push forward everyday knowing criticism, failures, old age, and death are unavoidable. It is my duty as a warrior to face the future with inner peace, equanimity, and infinite courage."

When a crab tries to climb out of a barrel, other crabs will try to grab on and pull it back down.

Similarly, when you start to pursue your passions, the people closest to you will be very uncomfortable and may try to hold you back.

If you let them, your family and friends will see your changes and subconsciously try to sabotage you by planting seeds of doubt in your psyche. They will oppose your changes with every fiber of their being. You were once a reflection of them, and if you change, they'll also have to change or get left behind. When you go after your dreams, people around you may start to feel inadequate. They'll want you to stop chasing your dreams because you make them reflect on all they *should be* doing with their lives.

When this happens, you will have two choices: You can either continue to awaken your warrior and love them from afar, or you can stop your awakening and go back to being mediocre in order to make others happy. So what will you choose? I certainly hope it's the former.

You want me to let you in on a little secret? People will never be happy because of something you do or don't do for them. The happiness or unhappiness of others really has nothing to do with you! Rise about the trivial opinions.

When working towards your goals, you will most certainly experience failures. Will you take your failures as lessons to learn from? Or will you fold, go home, and start being mediocre again? Again, I hope it's the former.

Old age and death will surely come. Are you scared? Do their impending visits cripple you and stop you from achieving your purpose? I most certainly hope not.

I see death as a blessing. It reminds me to go faster and push harder. I have to give five hundred, thousand, million, billion, *gazillion* percent every single day because death is always waiting. Death is here to tell us that we won't live forever. And if I'm not here forever, then I have a limited amount of time to do my life's work. And if I have a limited amount of time to do my life's work, then what the fuck am I waiting for? None of us have time for fear, mediocrity, or not realizing our purposes in life. Get to work!

We know criticism, failure, old age, and death are inevitable. But you are a warrior! Abandon fear and face them with inner peace, equanimity, and infinite courage!

Live Your Dream

"I'm committed to living full and dying empty."

A few years ago, I heard Les Brown say, “Live full, die empty.” Man, that really resonated with me! As soon as I heard him say that, I realized I wasn't giving my all to the pursuit of my happiness and goals. I was leaving gas in my tank.

Whether it be in jiu jitsu, love, business, or my health, I was always leaving something behind in my gas tank for the next day. But Les Brown reminded me that the more you give in your pursuits, the more you get *from* your pursuits. From then on, I’ve committed to going as hard as I can for as long as I can!

I’m committed to living full and dying empty. I'm going to ride it until the wheels fall off! I have no fear of death, and I know everything will work out exactly as it’s supposed to.

I will live full and die empty in everything I do. Will you?

Awakening the Warrior within Others

"I know it is my duty to raise the levels of consciousness of those I encounter on my journey, but only if they give me the permission to do so."

Your levels of consciousness will rise as you continue to achieve self-mastery and awaken the warrior within. "Level of consciousness" is just another way of saying your "level of awareness" or your "awakeness." Most of society is mindlessly sleepwalking, stuck in their own thoughts. You, my friend, will be different.

As you raise your levels of consciousness and engage in regular periods of self-reflection, you'll begin to alter your internal dialogue. After altering your internal dialogue, you'll alter your actions and dialogue with others.

It's an incredible thing that happens: You'll start to see opportunities you never noticed, but were always there. You'll meet the people whose goals are intertwined with yours in some way, and you'll help each other realize your dreams.

You'll discover the books, courses, and information you've been looking for your whole life, though you may not have even known you'd been looking. You used to not know what you didn't know, but now you know where your ignorance lies. Eventually, you'll be well-versed on every bit of information that will help fulfill your purpose.

As an incredible, physical and spiritual being living on this planet, it is your duty to raise your level of consciousness and awaken the warrior within yourself.

I know this sounds like a huge responsibility, may be difficult to believe, and I probably sound like a crazy person saying this, but know that you are made from all the pieces of the universe. Believe me. You're made from the same stuff as the cosmos and everything else on this planet. You owe it to the universe to be your very best self.

As you become more aware, you'll be able to practically read others' thoughts through their body language and expressions. Besides your duty to yourself and the universe to raise your levels of consciousness, you also owe it to other willing people to help raise *their* levels of consciousness.

It will be very tempting to immediately start coaching people on what they need to do to positively change their lives. I understand your desire to help others. I've been there. But I advise against trying to help people who reject or don't ask for your help. You'll seem like an arrogant asshole trying to force your beliefs on others.

Whenever I learned something new, I'd try to teach it to everyone. Most of my friends and family thought I was a lunatic for all my crazy ideas! People are scared of new things, or things that push them out of their comfort zones. New ideas, new exercises, new activities, new thoughts, and new belief systems terrify most people. You typically have to be very salesman-like and methodical in your approach when convincing people to try something new.

People will also think you're a pompous prick who doesn't accept them for who they are if you try to force change. I've gotten into debates and arguments about forcing new ideas on family and friends. This is not the way to help others. Be careful not to make the same mistakes I made in the past.

There's a method to the madness of introducing new things to people you love or want to help. The most important thing to remember is that you must stay present and alert in your conversations. Stay cognizant of what people are saying and doing, their body language, and even their thoughts.

First, surprise people with your attentiveness. Practice your listening skills. Put away your phone, turn off your TV, stop fidgeting, focus on your breathing, and just listen! Don't simply wait for your moment to speak like everyone else. *Listen!* This may take a lot of practice, but it'll be worth it in the end. People will trust you and will be open to hearing what you have to say after seeing how giving you are of your time and undivided attention.

Next, wait for an opportune moment. Wait for the moment people start to let their guards down and open up to you. Think of everything they've said, and pick up on something, anything you can help them with. Then say, "Jenny or Bob, may I teach you something?" Boom. Get people to trust and confide in you, then ask for permission to help then. People will be less inclined to fight and more open to your teachings. How incredible is that? Use this method in lieu of shoving your teachings down people's throats. You'll gain many more students and help to change many more lives this way.

Work on yourself, and offer to help others raise their consciousness levels. In turn, the people you help will help others. It'll be something like we've never seen before. People all over the planet will find inner peace, be more productive, and walk in their purpose. We'll experience a profound dispersion of positivity as warriors are awakened all over the world.

One Last Thing…

I've provided you with a lot of what you'll need on your journey in this book, but there's always room to learn more!

Visit **www.RomeZa.com to** learn about my seminars/workshops, speaking engagements, home study courses, and to view my newsletter. Would you like an even *more* personal touch? www.RomeZa.com is also the place to learn about my retreats and one-on-one coaching sessions. I want to do all I can to help unleash your greatness, but you've got to meet me halfway.

So, again, what are you waiting for?

Visit www.RomeZa.com today!

This book is a recorded history of my successes, failures, and lessons learned from the last few years. This is a history of the thousands of books I've read, the dozens of courses I've taken, and the many, many coaching programs I've done. It's a testimonial borne with self-reflection, pain, and struggle. I'm very grateful for all of the opportunities and challenges the universe has presented to me, and I'm thankful I get to share them with you.

As I reflect on my story up to this point, I'm reminded of a quote from The Teachings of Buddha: "Thousands of candles can be lighted from a single candle, and the life of the single candle will not be shortened. Happiness never decreases by being shared." I lose nothing from helping others, and I gain the satisfaction of knowing I've helped someone start a purposeful journey. I want to share my story with you. I want to connect with you in hopes of helping you avoid some of the pitfalls I fell into as I awakened the warrior within. I lay myself bare before you, dear reader. Keep my words in mind as you awaken your warrior and consciously evolve on your path to success.

An Entrepreneur, Visionary, and Coach committed to helping you step into your GREATNESS and Awaken the WARRIOR within you...

Made in the USA
Lexington, KY
20 August 2017